FLYING CRANE

108 Haiku and Senryu

Tsanka Shishkova

Copyright© 2021 Tsanka Shishkova
ISBN: 978-81-8253-758-3

First Edition: 2021
Rs. 200/-

Cyberwit.net
HIG 45 Kaushambi Kunj, Kalindipuram
Allahabad - 211011 (U.P.) India
http://www.cyberwit.net
Tel: +(91) 9415091004
E-mail: info@cyberwit.net

Printed at Repro India Limited.

1

sazanka shining
in the hand of Buddha
snow moon

2

sunny day
white puppy marvels
at the snowflakes

3

pink moon
across the universe
midnight jazz

4

lockdown
bird feeding station
in the courtyard

5

late autumn
shadows of bare branches
paint the road

6

mom's lazy chair...
still hear
her fairy tales

7

tea plantation
a hundred shades
of green
NHK WORLD-JAPAN, HAIKU MASTERS program, 2018,
July

8

dark clouds
lightning flashes lit up
a flower
Mamba, Afrika Haiku Network, Issue 2, 2016

9
pink moon...
crane feather on
the cherry tree
ASAHI HAIKUIST NETWORK, April 5, 2019

10
baby's curls
I'm trying to draw
an enso
ASAHI HAIKUIST NETWORK, 1 January 2021

11
worm moon
on the roof pretty cat
and two tomcats
ASAHI HAIKUIST NETWORK/ David McMurray, March
06, 2020

12
equinox ...
on the clock tower
a new nest
ASAHI HAIKUIST NETWORK/ David McMurray, March
20, 2020

13

bonfire
in the mountain meadow
the scent of mursala tea
ASAHI HAIKUIST NETWORK/ David McMurray, April 17,
2020

14

a woman without a dog ...
yet, blooming sakura
is not alone
ASAHI HAIKUIST NETWORK/ David McMurray, May 29,
2020

15

pandemic moon ... alone with a cup of green tea
ASAHI HAIKUIST NETWORK/ David McMurray, June 05,
2020

16

cleans weeds around the rose The Little Prince
ASAHI HAIKUIST NETWORK/ David McMurray, June 05,
2020

17
boats and fires
on the night of July
cormorant fishing
ASAHI HAIKUIST NETWORK/ David McMurray, June 19,
2020

18
summertime
in the moonlight
lilies bloom
ASAHI HAIKUIST NETWORK/ David McMurray, 3 July,
2020

19
cold moon
Christmas fireplace burning
in the wanderer's dream
ASAHI HAIKUIST NETWORK/ David McMurray, January
03, 2020

20
diary book
with a map of Japan—
Christmas gift
ASAHI HAIKUIST NETWORK/ David McMurray, March
06, 2020

21
rush hour ...
cherries must be blooming
somewhere
ASAHI HAIKUIST NETWORK/ David McMurray, April 17,
2020

22
beach temple ...
near the stone garden
wind flutes
ASAHI HAIKUIST NETWORK/ David McMurray, 17 July
2020

23
Aegean island
reflections of white houses
in the sea
ASAHI HAIKUIST NETWORK/ David McMurray, 21
August, 2020

24
aroma of home
flowering chestnuts
after the rain
ASAHI HAIKUIST NETWORK/ David McMurray, 4
September, 2020

25
heat
new anthill
in the garden
ASAHI HAIKUIST NETWORK/ David McMurray, 4
September, 2020

26
social distance
under the shooting stars
tender hug
ASAHI HAIKUIST NETWORK/ David McMurray, 2
October 2020

27
sand mandala
created by the universe
and so, destructed
ASAHI HAIKUIST NETWORK/ David McMurray, 16
October, 2020

28
a cup of tea ...
I miss you
in late autumn
ASAHI HAIKUIST NETWORK/ David McMurray, 16
October, 2020

29
homecoming...
the lonely ghost of
my childhood
ASAHI HAIKUIST NETWORK/ David McMurray, 30
October, 2020

30
storm
ghosts of felled trees
groan and weep
ASAHI HAIKUIST NETWORK/ David McMurray, 6
November 2020

31
glass plate
with apples and rose hips
cranes fly south
ASAHI HAIKUIST NETWORK/ David McMurray, 4
December 2020

32
new moon...
in the river plum petals
and stars
ASAHI HAIKUIST NETWORK/ David McMurray, May 3,
2019

33
a gentle breeze
brings the scent of spring
plums on the hill
ASAHI HAIKUIST NETWORK/ David McMurray, 2 April
2021

34
time traveler
getting old imperceptibly
but it's still tempting
ASAHI HAIKUIST NETWORK/ David McMurray, 19 April
2021

35
Insomnia
song of nightingales
before dawn
ASAHI HAIKUIST NETWORK/ David McMurray, 19 April
2021

36
one more haiku
dedicated to my son
blooming irises
ASAHI HAIKUIST NETWORK/ David McMurray, accepted

37
stars so bright
on winter night garden
camellia shines
ESUJ-H, English Haiku, February, 2020

38
two evening stars
over the blooming trees . . .
Beethoven on my playlist
ESUJ-H, English Haiku, April, 2020

39
distant thunder...
in the moonlit river
blooming lilies
ESUJ-H, English Haiku, June, 2020

40
color therapy
in the hospital
coral garden
ESUJ-H, English Haiku, August, 2020

41
dawn
in the icicle
rainbows
UTB 2020 - MODERN HAIKU

42
autumn
our last day
together
UTB 2020 - - HAIGA & VISUAL HAIKU

43
sunrise
distant lightning
blows up the sky
UTB 2020 - HAIBUN

44
heritage
handwritten letters in
handmade box
UTB 2020 - POET'S PERSONAL BEST

45
stardust
on snowy roads –
Godspeed
Stardust Haiku, issue 36

46
glass wind chimes...
the sounds
of my childhood
Stardust Haiku, issue 37

47
insomnia...
even Sirius
doesn't shine
Stardust Haiku, issue 38

48
Mozart ...
needing
no translation
Stardust Haiku, issue 40

49

pandemic moon...
nothing
but a blues song
Stardust Haiku, issue 41

50

midnight jazz
the sense
of the universe
Stardust Haiku, issue 42

51
walking alone
along the sea
pandemic night
Stardust Haiku, issue 43

52
art gallery
of our family tree
grandma's attic
Stardust Haiku, issue 44

53
tears
on the ticket
long flight
Stardust Haiku, issue 47

54
campfire
under the African moon
colorful dancer
The Mamba, Africa's haiku journal, Issue 9

55
high tide
on the walking path cockle
shells
The Mamba, Africa's haiku journal, Issue 10

56
five pm
one more
teatime story
The Mamba, Africa's haiku journal, Issue 11

57

no sharp stones in the sea an old sailors' song
The Mamba, Africa's haiku journal, Issue 11

58

winter
in summer colors
hat and scarf
Failed Haiku, Issue 49

59
late autumn
still feeling the spirit
of spring
Failed Haiku, Issue 49

60
abandoned home
but swallows
in their nests
FemkuMag, April, 2021

61
footbridge
covered with autumn leaves
water lily pond
Autumn Moon Haiku Journal, Autumn – Winter 2020-2021

62
sunny afternoon
on a bench facing the sun
autumn leaves
Autumn Moon Haiku Journal, Autumn – Winter 2020-2021

63
snowstorm
in the apple tree
chanting bells
Autumn Moon Haiku Journal, Autumn – Winter 2020-2021

64
cosmic sounds
in moonless night
music of Bach
Cold Moon Journal, February 13, 2021

65
moonlit silence
shared loneliness
with a cup of tea
Cold Moon Journal, February 18, 2021

66
alone
with flowering plum
social distance
Cold Moon Journal, February 19, 2021

67
'stay at home'
they say again and again
my kite stays in the box
Cold Moon Journal, February 20, 2021

68
I follow the sound
of the temple bell
heavy fog
Cold Moon Journal, March 7, 2021

69
three-line poems
in the pandemic-time
haiku therapy
Cold Moon Journal, April 16, 2021

70
universe
in a candle burning time
meditation

71

old cathedral
earthly and divine
in perfect harmony

72

winding path
moonless night but the light
of temple lanterns

73

anniversary
walk among the azaleas
in grandma's garden

74

the storm is over
pink lotus reblooms
with sunrise

75
back in the '60s
sing and dance at a rock concert
as you can

76
SMS
for canceling a wedding
pandemic lockdown

77
home
the comfort of
my mess

78
abandoned house
at the doorstep
cat with kittens

79
red roses
on the grave
mom's birthday

80
alone in the silence
of the sea breeze ...
a song of fisherman

81
sound
of the universe
Bach's music

82
open window
my paper crane
flies off

83
first date
social distance
between them

84
zoom party
newborn baby
in the family

85
sunflower
star mandala
in my mind

86
lark song
at the sunlit dawn
distant thunder

87
jasmine
the same scent
everywhere

88
sound of seagulls
and the salty smell
summer by the sea

89
online meeting
dad presents updates
of the family tree

90
earthquake...
on a broken stained glass
Virgin Mary

91
blooming lilies
on the moonlit river
distant thunder

92
rainy days
carpets of wildflowers
in the desert

93
moonless night
in the temple's pond
lilies and stars

94
harvest moon
brighter is the light
of your soul

95
path of lights
toward my home
holy Diwali

96
shining
snowflakes
rising sun

97
rocky path
blown by the wind
a touch of the sea

98
Perseids…
tides wash away
our trace

99
sand lily
behind the dunes
sea-level rise

100
blue pearl
in a small blue mussel
high tide

101
sherpas
on the way to the top
indigo children

102
rising sun
shining petals
on my way

103
bird feeders
on the porch
social distance

104
traveler's moon
the lighthouse lights
a coming storm

105
pealing thunders...
lightning lights up
apple flowers

106
unsent letter
song of nightingales
before dawn

107
Camino de Santiago
thousands of prayers
across the universe

108
elderly couple
dancing outdoor
pink moon